North Yorkshire Moors Railway

**A Pictorial Survey
compiled by David Joy**

**Dalesman Books
1987**

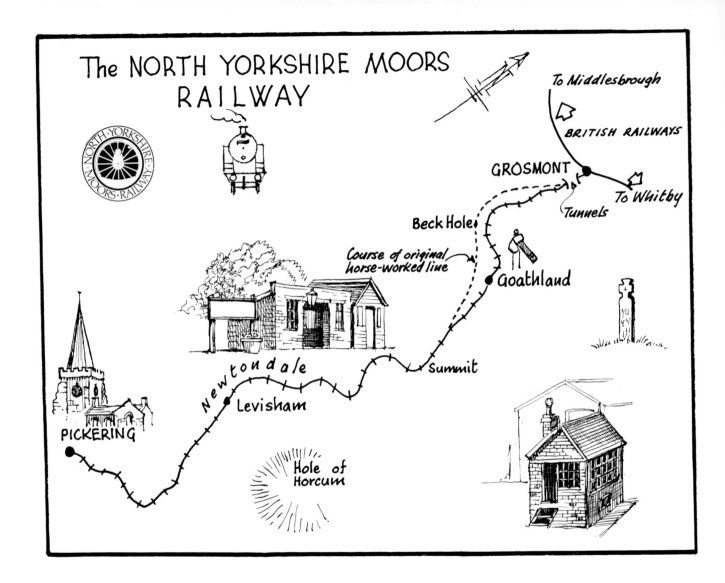

The NORTH YORKSHIRE MOORS RAILWAY

To Middlesbrough

BRITISH RAILWAYS

GROSMONT

To Whitby

Tunnels

Beck Hole

Course of original horse-worked line

Goathland

Newtondale

Summit

Levisham

PICKERING

Hole of Horcum

CONTENTS

Cover photographs:-
Front: No. 3180 'Antwerp' storms past Esk Valley on the climb to Goathland
(*Mrs D. A. Robinson*).
Back: No. 5690 'Leander' near Beckhole (*Maurice Burns*).

The Dalesman Publishing Company Ltd, Clapham, Lancaster, LA2 8EB

© Text, David Joy, 1987

ISBN: 0 85206 904 9

Printed by Smiths of Bradford, Bradford, West Yorkshire

Introduction

THE North Yorkshire Moors Railway has many claims to fame. It is one of the longest privately operated railways in Britain, running for almost its entire 138 miles through superb National Park scenery. It offers a magnificent stomping ground for its wide-ranging collection of steam locomotives. It caters for the needs of the community and the economy of the area by providing a regular train service, and it offers an outlet for the hundreds of young people who have gathered together to help in running a railway.

The line is also one of the earliest and most historic in the north of England. Its origins go back almost a century and a half to 1832 when the coastal town of Whitby was becoming increasingly concerned about the decline in its staple industries of whaling, shipbuilding and alum working. There was a general feeling that trade would improve if better inland communications could be provided, and so a local committee asked no less an authority than George Stephenson to report on builiding a railway "of simplest construction for the employment of animal power". He advised that a line to Pickering "would amply remunerate the proprietors for the money invested" by transporting coal and other sea-borne goods inland to the Vale of Ryedale and, in the opposite direction, conveying agricultural produce and building stone to Whitby for shipment.

Fired by this optimism, the promoters obtained an Act of Parliament on May 6th, 1833, and construction of the single-line horse-worked Whitby & Pickering Railway was put in hand. From a terminus alongside the harbour at Whitby it crossed the river Esk nine times before reaching Grosmont and a short tunnel which took the line into the valley of the Murk Esk. Perhaps the most remarkable feature of the railway was at Beckhole where a 1,500ft long rope-worked incline with a maximum gradient of 1 in 10 preceded the approach to the upland village of Goathland. Still climbing, the line reached a summit level of over 500ft at accurately named Fen Bog before entering the magnificent glacial gorge of Newtondale which provided a gradually descending natural routeway right through to Pickering.

Regular passenger services between Whitby and Grosmont began on June 8th, 1835, but not until May 26th, 1836, was the line formally opened throughout amid great celebrations with brass bands playing, church bells pealing and cannon firing. It soon transformed the local economy, despite the fact that it took passengers almost 2½ hours to cover the 24 miles from Whitby to Pickering in carriages which, apart from flanged wheels, made no concessions to evolution from the stagecoach. The railway had cost £105,000, more than double the original estimate, and remained financially weak until it was rescued from isolation and penury by George Hudson, the "railway king", who decided to connect it to the expanding national rail network and develop Whitby as a holiday resort. In 1844 his York and North Midland Railway began to build lines from York to Scarborough and Pickering, and in the following year purchased the Whitby line for £80,000 – £25,000 less than it cost to construct – and started to convert it into a double-track route suitable for locomotive haulage. This work was complete by July 1847 when steam trains entered Whitby for the first time.

Two years later came Hudson's fall from power, and in 1854 the line became part of the newly formed North Eastern Railway. As traffic developed the rope-worked incline proved to be an increasing handicap. There were odorous complications when a train loaded with herrings ran away, and matters came to a head with a fatal accident in 1864. By this time a difficult 4½ mile deviation line running on a 1 in 49 gradient from Grosmont to Moorgates was being completed at a cost of £50,000 and, along with a new station at Goathland, was opened on July 1st, 1865. In the same year Grosmont became a junction with the completion of the Esk Valley route from Middlesbrough.

The line then passed through a century of relatively uneventful existence until its rural tranquility was shattered by a bombshell in the shape of the Beeching Report which proposed the closure of all railways into Whitby. The Esk Valley route was ultimately reprieved, but harsh economics gained a shallow victory over social necessity on March 8th, 1965, when the Pickering line was closed from its junction with the York - Scarborough route at Rillington through to Grosmont. British Railways claimed an annual loss of £50,000 was being incurred, but many local folk were convinced that the line could be viable if run with voluntary help. The upshot was some well-supported public meetings in 1967 which led to the formation of first the North Yorkshire Moors Railway Preservation Society and then a separate company to negotiate with British Railways. Owing to the high costs involved the initial intention was to buy just the section of line from Grosmont to Ellerbeck, near the summit, for £35,000, but then fortunes changed when the old North Riding County Council and the English Tourist Board began to take an interest in the proposals. It was felt that, as the railway offered the best access to unique Newtondale, its retention would be preferable to the alternative of having narrow roads choked with motor traffic. Thus, at the eleventh hour the County Council provided the financial springboard for purchase right through to Pickering.

In 1971 the line achieved another record when it became the first operating railway to achieve charitable status. The assets of both the preservation society and the company were transferred to the North York Moors Historical Railway Trust Ltd., which has as its aims "to advance the education of the public in the history and development of railway locomotion by the maintenance in working order of the historic and scenic railway line between the towns of Grosmont and Pickering". Although it was possible to run trains from 1970, public reopening was delayed by the legal complexities in obtaining the necessary Light Railway Orders. Passenger services were finally resumed on April 22nd, 1973, and then on May 1st came the line's red letter day with the formal and royal reopening by the Duchess of Kent. The railway has since gone from strength to strength, attacting increasing numbers of visitors who come to see the growing array of steam locomotives and the superb scenery.

The present-day flavour of the line has been well summarised by Michael Pitts, chairman of the North York Moors Historical Railway Trust. In a foreword to *Steam on the North York Moors,* a guide to the line and an essential companion to the present volume, he comments: "Today the NYMR is a railway thriving as never before in its history. Annual totals of passenger journeys are measured in hundreds of thousands – old folk re-living their memories, families on their first ever train trip, school parties studying geology or ecology or history, diners enjoying Pullman service, excited children on Santa Specials, railway enthusiasts photographing and sound-recording the performances of particular locomotives . . . The main key to the NYMR's steady growth has been the dedication and fellowship of its staff – full time, seasonal and volunteer. A working historic railway involves much more than just running a time-tabled service. Locomotives and carriages have been restored; track, bridges and fences have been maintained and improved; new passing loops and sidings have been laid. But much remains to be done. Indeed the tasks will be never-ending if the NYMR is going to flourish until its bi-centenary in 2036 and beyond".

George Stephenson to Doctor Beeching

130 Years of Change 1835 – 1965

The spirit and atmosphere of the original horse-worked line was well captured in a series of engravings by George Dodgson, a noted watercolourist. These formed part of a book, 'The Scenery of Whitby and Pickering Railway', published in 1836 to commemorate the opening of the line. Here, passengers in Newtondale are seen hailing the coach during stormy weather.

The engraving above depicts the fragile wooden bridge across the Murk Esk at Grosmont and the distinctive tunnel with its castellated and turreted portal. When the line was converted to locomotive haulage in 1847, a new double-track tunnel was built and the original structure allowed to remain (top, right). Today it forms a vital link between Grosmont station and the locomotive shed (*Peter Williams*). The other engraving (right) shows a first-class coach at the summit of the line.

Between Grosmont and Moorgates, south of Goathland, the original route ran on a completely different course which included a rope-worked incline ascending at 1 in 10 from the hamlet of Beckhole. This survived until 1865 when it was replaced by a 1 in 49 deviation line with a new station at Goathland, seen here in 1939. Note on the extreme right the stone crusher which was served by a narrow-gauge tramway from Silhowe (*Locomotive & General Railway Photographs*).

In 1908 the original route was reopened as far as Beckhole for summer services which survived until 1914. Here the inaugural train is seen at the terminus (*collection of Mrs. G. E. Deakin*).

THE CHANGING SCENE. Both present-day termini of the North Yorkshire Moors Railway have completely altered in appearance down the years. At Grosmont the station was at one time dominated by an ironworks which was in blast from about 1863 until 1891 - all traces of it have now disappeared (*The Sutcliffe Gallery*).

At Pickering a regrettable change was the removal of the overall roof in 1953. It dated from 1845 when George Hudson took over the Whitby & Pickering Railway and connected it to his York-Scarborough line by building a branch from Rillington, near Malton. The station was designed by G. T. Andrews, who was Sheriff of York at the same time as Hudson was Lord Mayor. D49 No. 62726 is preparing to depart with an up train about 1949 (*W. A. Camwell*).

A characteristic inter-war scene on the line. A begrimed 4-6-2T No. 688, banked in the rear, is storming out of Grosmont with the morning Whitby-Leeds train in August 1939. Note the lower quadrant signals and the motley collection of rolling stock (*J. W. Armstrong*).

Major transformation came to the line from 1958 with the introduction of diesel multiple units which took over most of the local services. This wintry scene shows a down train pausing at a noticeably deserted Goathland station (*Tindale's of Whitby*).

Diesel-hauled passenger train passing Goathland summit in snowy conditions. Lack of traffic in the winter months was a factor which precipitated the line's closure in March 1965 under the ravages of the Beeching Plan (*Maurice Burns*).

The Preservation Era

Negotiations involving the formation of the North Yorkshire Moors Railway were protracted, and almost four years elapsed after closure before crowds assembled at Goathland on a wintry February 2nd, 1969, to see 0-4-0ST 'Mirvale' making the preservation society's first train movement. The locomotive was en route from Pickering to Grosmont (*Tindale's of Whitby*).

IMPROVISATION. In a situation reminiscent of 'The Titfield Thunderbolt' film classic, 'Salmon' makes an emergency stop for bucket-chain refreshment during its journey from Pickering to Grosmont on March 30th, 1969. Such problems were not uncommon in the first haltering phase of the line's re-birth (*John M. Boyes*).

Another difficulty of the early days was that coaling at Grosmont station had to be undertaken manually. Notice the sheet draped over the bunker side to protect the locomotive paintwork and the empty sacks hanging on the level crossing gate on the left (*Peter Williams*).

14　　**Red-letter day. The royal train conveying the Duchess of Kent steams into Grosmont on the official re-opening of the line on May 1st, 1973 (*John Hunt*).**

Another regal occasion - the Queen's silver jubilee in 1977 - saw this magnificently bedecked special about to depart from Grosmont for Pickering on June 7th (*Maurice Burns*).

15

Footplate portrait - Driver Terry Newman (right) and Fireman Maurice Burns on the K1 No. 2005 (*John Hunt*).

THE DAILY ROUND. One is never short of a job on the North Yorkshire Moors line. Young volunteers (left) chat with guard and ticket inspector, the Rev. R. Chadwick, as he checks their tickets (*David Idle*). By contrast (right), there is always somthing to be kept tidy, right down to flowers growing in a surplus locomotive chimney (*Peter Williams*).

Left: The North Yorkshire Moors Railway has had a succession of visiting locomotives down the years. One of the most distinctive has been Great Northern Railway Stirling No. 1, seen approaching Levisham during BBC TV filming in 1986 (*Maurice Burns*).

Right: Jubilee No. 5690 'Leander' visited the line in 1983, when it was photographed in July climbing past Green End towards Goathland (*Mrs D. A. Robinson*).

Right: Named trains have featured on the line virtually since reopening. K1 No. 2005 is entering Goathland with 'The Moorlander' in May 1979 (*David Idle*).

Left: Out-of-season operations include the well-patronised Santa specials. J72 No. 69023 'Joem' was climbing towards Goathland with one such special in December 1984 (*Peter J. Robinson*).

Right: Other unconventional specials have included 'A Midsummer Night's Steam', chartered by Whitbread Breweries on June 24th, 1981, as a fundraiser for the Licensed Victuallers' National Homes. This 11.00pm view shows No 4767 at Pickering about to work the empty stock back to Grosmont (*John Barry*).

One of the great success stories of the line has been the North Yorkshire Pullman, making a return journey from Pickering or Grosmont on summer evenings. Passengers enjoy luxury accommodation in the Parlour Cars 'Opal' and 'Garnet' and the Kitchen Car 'Robin', and the culinary delights of a five-course dinner freshly prepared on the train. The Pullman is seen here in Newtondale in charge of D9529 in April 1984 (*David Idle*).

NORTH YORKSHIRE PULLMAN

TRAVEL IN PULLMAN LUXURY ON THE
NORTH YORKSHIRE MOORS RAILWAY
AND ENJOY THE CULINARY DELIGHTS
OF DINNER ON THE TRAIN

MENU

Barquette d'Ananas
Pâté de Campagne avec Baguette

*   *   *

Velouté Andaloux
Consommé Xérès

*   *   *

Sorbet Citron

*   *   *

Suprême de Volaille en Croûte Florentin
Contre-Filet de Boeuf Chasseur
Sélection de Légumes

*   *   *

Tarte aux Pommes
Bavarois aux Fruits

*   *   *

Crêpe Suzette
(supplement £5.00 per person)

*   *   *

Café

£18.00

Please let us know on booking if vegetarian dishes are required

The mouth-watering menu of the North Yorkshire Pullman. How can any passenger fail to be tempted by such delicacies?

Along the Line

Although rather more than half the passengers on the North Yorkshire Moors Railway now start their journey at Pickering, Grosmont boasts the main locomotive shed and thus remains the operational departure point. This photo-tour of the line therefore starts at Grosmont station, with its distinctive architecture and platform accessories (*Peter Williams*).

Much activity at Grosmont at Easter 1985. J72 No. 69023 'Joem' acts as station pilot, while K1 No. 2005 departs with a Pickering train (*Maurice Burns*).

Left: Driver's eye view from a locomotive about to leave Grosmont and head through the double-track tunnel (*Peter Williams*).

Right: At the south end of Grosmont tunnel are the locomotive sheds. 5MT No. 5428 'Eric Treacy' is passing 'Joem' and the K1 in August 1984 (*Peter J. Robinson*).

Left: From just outside Grosmont the line climbs for three miles to Goathland on a continuous gradient of 1 in 49 which taxes locomotives to the utmost and provides for some spectacular smoke and sound effects. 0-6-2T No. 29 is passing Esk Valley in the early stages of the climb, back in the pioneering days of operations in the summer of 1975 (*John Hunt*).

Right: Further up the grade at Beckhole, P3 No. 2392 is in charge of a diminutive freight during a steam gala in May 1977 (*Peter J. Robinson*).

Left: Trains are regularly scheduled to pass at Goathland. No. D821 'Greyhound' is waiting at the up platform in summer 1982 for K1 No. 2005 to arrive with a train from Pickering (*Mrs D. A. Robinson*).

Right: The signal-box at Goathland is a cosy building of great character. 0-6-2T No. 29 brings its coaches into the platform, while a youthful helper stands ready to exchange tokens with the crew in accordance with the normal practice of single-line working (*Peter Williams*).

Right: The 21-lever frame inside the box controls all signals and points within the station limits. In the high season with up and down trains crossing, passengers changing platforms and locomotives running round trains, the signalman is kept very busy indeed (*Peter Williams*).

31

Newtondale Halt (above), deep in the depths of the gorge, was officially opened by Hector Monro, Minister for Sport, on June 15th, 1981. A joint venture by the railway, the North York Moors National Park and the Countryside and Forestry Commissions, it gives the public access to a carefully planned network of paths in the quietude of the valley. The halt is possibly further away from a public highway than any other station in England. The view (left) shows refreshments being served at the Halt in July 1985. (*David Idle*).

Opposite:
After reaching the summit of almost 550ft above sea level the line enters the classic glacial overflow gorge of Newtondale which provides a superb background when photographing trains on the move. 0-6-2T No. 29 is heading a works train into the gorge at Easter 1973 (*John Hunt*).

Left: Levisham shares with Goathland the function of acting as a crossing-place for trains travelling in opposite directions. The first 'steam meet' there for 13 years saw 0-6-2T No. 29 on 'The Moorlander' pass P3 No. 2392 on 'The North Yorkshireman' at Whitsuntide 1975 (*John Hunt*).

Right: Bird's eye view of the line snaking its way through the magnificent Newtondale gorge. (*Mick Roberts*).

Right: No. D821 'Greyhound' in
Newtondale with a Grosmont - Pickering
train in August 1982 (*Peter J. Robinson*).

Left: After 17 miles the railway finally
leaves the Newtondale gorge and
approaches civilisation at New Bridge
Crossing where the road from Pickering
to Newton and Stape straddles the line.
The interior of New Bridge signal-box
controls the whole of the Pickering end of
the line by means of colour-light signals
and power-operated points. Note the
Tyler's Patent token apparatus for
single-line working (*Murray Brown*).

Left: Pickering station, now forming the
administrative headquarters of the
railway, has never visually recovered
from the amputation of its overall roof.
The cantilever canopies are out of
keeping with the remaining architecture,
but the stonework itself is of a high
quality and well repays close study
(*John Hunt*).

Steam Locomotives

Above: Some of the locomotives active on the line are appropriately enough ex North Eastern Railway. P3 No. 2392 has been superbly restored by the North Eastern Locomotive Preservation Group; it is seen passing Beckhole with a pick-up freight in November 1971 (*John Hunt*).

Left: Another magnificent NELPG engine is T2 0-8-0 No. 2238, built at Darlington in 1918. In October 1981 it was putting up an impressive smoke screen as it climbed out of Goathland (*John Hunt*).

Although of North Eastern Railway design, class J72 0-6-0T No. 69023 'Joem' was built at Darlington as late as 1951. Shortly after its arrival on the North Yorkshire Moors Railway, it is seen double-heading a train for Pickering near Beckhole (*Maurice Burns*).

No. 2005 was built in 1949 by the North British Locomotive Company in Glasgow. Withdrawn in 1967, it was immaculately restored by the North Eastern Locomotive Preservation Group in LNER apple green livery and is seen here at Pickering in 1982 (*David Idle*).

LMS 5MT No. 4767 was built at Crewe in 1947 and came to the line in 1974. In the view above it is about to depart from Goathland with a Grosmont train in July 1981. The locomotive, which has unique Stephenson link motion, was named 'George Stephenson' in 1975 by William Whitelaw, M.P., son of a former chairman of the LNER it is seen opposite climbing through Newtondale with a train for Grosmont in August 1980 (*David Idle; Peter Williams; Maurice Burns*).

Another ex-LMS locomotive, Jubilee No. 5690 'Leander', departing from Goathland with a Pickering train on June 20th, 1983 (*Maurice Burns*).

Sister Engine on the line to 'George Stephenson', No. 5428 was built at Newcastle in 1937 and withdrawn in 1967. The locomotive arrived on the North Yorkshire Moors Railway in 1973 and is seen here leaving Grosmont tunnel in August 1975. It has been named 'Eric Treacy' after the former Bishop of Wakefield, a noted railway photographer (*J. H. Cooper-Smith*).

Left: BR class 4MT No. 80135, built at Brighton as late as 1956, had only a short working life before being condemned to Barry scrapyard. Retrieved and transported to the North Yorkshire Moors line following a £5,000 appeal, it was restored and entered service in 1980. Here it is shown struggling up the last few yards of the 1 in 49 into Goathland with a heavily-clinkered fire; Deltic diesel No. 55019 is providing rear-end assistance (*Maurice Burns*).

Right: Great Western Railway 0-6-2T No. 6619 was purchased from Barry scrapyard in 1975, its restoration being completed ten years later. In July 1985 it was storming through Newtondale with a ten-coach train (*Mick Roberts*).

Ex-Southern Railway No. 841 'Greene King' was built at Eastleigh in 1936 as one of the S15 class designed by R. E. L. Maunsell. Taken out of service in 1964, she was rescued from Barry scrapyard eight years later and after a period on the Nene Valley Railway came to Grosmont in 1978. The 'King' is seen at Levisham in August 1979 (*David Idle*).

Ex-LNER class J94 No. 3180 'Antwerp', on loan from the National Coal Board, made its first run on the railway in September 1980, and entered regular service after being officially renamed on April 26th, 1981. Here it is climbing past Green End with a lightweight train from Grosmont to Goathland (*David Addyman*).

The newest of the industrial locomotives on the line is 0-6-0ST No. 47 'Moorbarrow', the product of Robert Stephenson & Hawthorns Ltd in 1955. Most of its short working life was spent on the Backworth colliery lines in Northumberland, the engine being purchased by Longlands College Locomotive Society at Middlesbrough in 1973 and moved to Pickering station five years later. It is named after a fictional community based on Goathland and created by local authoress Pat Wilson (*Peter Williams*).

0-6-2T No. 29 'Lambton' was built by Kitson of Leeds in 1904 for the Lambton, Hetton & Joicey Collieries in County Durham and was purchased from the National Coal Board in 1970 for transfer to the 'Moorsline'. In green livery, lined in black and yellow, she carried more than her fair share of passengers in the early days of operations (*Peter Williams*).

Physically and historically closely related to No. 29, 0-6-2T No. 5 is five years the younger being constructed by Robert Stephenson Ltd of Darlington in 1909. Likewise purchased from the NCB in 1970, this engine also worked hard in the formative years to get the railway off to a good start. Initially turned out in unlined black livery, No. 5 was later given the red lining of North Eastern goods locomotives (*Peter Williams*).

0-6-0T No. 31 'Meteor' arrived on the line in 1973. Built by Robert Stephenson & Hawthorns Ltd in 1950, she had previously worked at various collieries in Northumberland. In August 1982 she was living up to her name as she burst forth from Grosmont tunnel with a morning train for Pickering (*Maurice Burns*).

Diesel Traction

A striking arrival in 1981 was No. D821 'Greyhound', seen at Levisham on April 21st when it hauled its first passenger trains over the route. A member of the 2,200h.p. Warship class, it was built at Swindon in 1960 and was purchased by the Diesel Traction Group following withdrawal in 1972. It was subsequently repainted in its original maroon livery and was latterly on display at Swindon Works (*David Idle*).

'Greyhound' journeyed north with the Diesel Traction Group's second acquisition, Hymek class 35 No. D7029, which on July 26th, 1981, was approaching Goathland with a well-filled afternoon train. Built by Beyer Peacock Ltd in 1962, it spent its entire life on the Western Region before being taken out of service in 1975. Following preservation, it has been repainted in two tone green livery (*David Chadwick*).

A pair of 'Deltics', among the most successful of all diesel locomotives, graced North Yorkshire Moors Railway metals from August 1982. No. 55009 'Alycidon' is departing from Goathland in April 1984 (*David Idle*).

Class 24 No. D5032 was built at Crewe in 1959. Sold in 1976 to scrap processors at Stockton, the engine was subsequently hired for use on the line during the drought of 1976 and has remained on loan ever since! 'Helen Turner', the name it received in 1982, is the daughter of the owning company's managing director. In July 1984 it was receiving a wash and brush-up at Pickering (*David Idle*).

No. 21 is a diesel-hydraulic 0-4-0 built by Fowler of Leeds in 1955. It is on loan from the British Steel Corporation and has a distinctive blue livery (*Peter Williams*).

Class 04 No. D2207 is a handy little machine, invaluable for such tasks as witnessed here on April 10th, 1982, when it was hauling empty stock from Goathland to Grosmont past Green End. Built by the Drewry Company in 1953, the engine was subsequently acquired for preservation in 1974 (*David Addyman*).

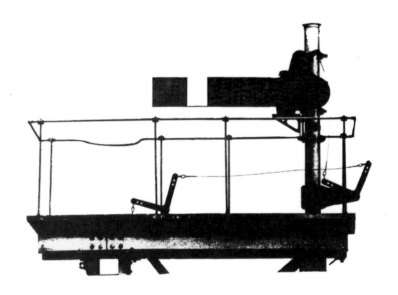